I0478436

Lyft Driving for Profit

A definitive guide to making money with ride share.

By, Richard Ramsey

Dedication

Special thanks to everyone that has ever set foot in my vehicle. After several thousand rides I have made some great friends, made some good money, and learned a lot about my city. I look forward to future rides and new adventures.

Table of Contents

Who should drive for Lyft?

Rideshare is not for everyone. Just because you have a car and license doesn't mean that you have what it takes to be successful in rideshare. It is much more complicated than simply turning on the app and driving as Lyft would have you believe. There is in fact an actual strategy to driving if you want to be successful.

Communication / Conversation

Driving is a critical component of Lyft, but what you are really providing while driving is an "experience". This is especially true when your passengers are new to Lyft, celebrating, or on vacation. You aren't just a driver, you are an entertainer, a tour guide, and at times even a counselor. This is where many taxi drivers fail. They don't understand that a typical Lyft passenger expects so much more from their driver than they do from a typical cabbie. WE are part of the experience, not just a means of getting to an experience. Part of this is because of the great past experiences riders have had with other drivers. A great driver creates greater expectations of future drivers. For this reason, you have to always be ready to be more than just a driver.

Understanding that we are MORE than just drivers means that we have to relate to our passengers on a personal level. This can only be done effectively if you are a good communicator. You have to know how to talk to people, what questions to ask, and how to generate conversation with a wide variety of people. There is nothing more uncomfortable than sitting in a stranger's vehicle in silence. If you aren't good at striking up conversation you aren't going to be successful with Lyft. It is the single most important factor (after driving) in determining whether you will get tips and in determining how well the rider will rate their experience.

If you were to ask your riders about their best Lyft experiences, the vast majority are going to tell you about drivers that made them laugh. If you ask about their worst experiences, they will talk about that driver that never said a word to them for thirty minutes. Conversation is critical! If you lack this ability consider Lyft Eats and other delivery services.

It is also equally important to realize that there can be too much of a good thing. If the rider is avoidant, has their headphones in, or is clearly engaged in something else, conversation isn't nearly as important. You want to make certain they know you are friendly and there for them without being overbearing and obnoxious. You have to read their verbal/non-verbal cues to know the best route to take with each rider.

Driving / Navigation

Driving is another important component of being an Lyft driver for obvious reasons. The problem is that many drivers assume this means simply staying in the lines and keeping the passenger alive. If you are going to drive for Lyft you HAVE TO understand what a passenger expects from their driver.

Passengers are going to look at the ride MUCH differently than the driver does. They aren't going to notice the traffic, but they will notice the time. They aren't going to notice the accidents you avoided, but they will notice that time you slammed on your breaks. You have to keep in mind that your perspective is much different than theirs.

A driver has to be able to not only get a passenger to their destination in a reasonable amount of time, they have to do so while driving safely. Your stops and accelerations must be smooth. Your speed must be normal (not too fast or too slow). You shouldn't change lanes frequently. Your entire goal should be to drive consistently. You have to remember that your rider knows nothing about you or your ability. All they know is that you are whipping through traffic like a racecar driver. Stay consistent, pick a lane, drive smoothly, and stay confident.

Another component of driving is your ability to navigate. This doesn't mean that you have to know the exact route to your destination. It means that you have to understand how to use technology to get you there. You have to pay attention to that technology and you have to be ready to change routes if something comes up such as an accident, road closure, etc. One of the biggest complaints I hear from riders about other drives is that they missed a turn, didn't go the way the rider wanted them to, or simply got lost. Use your GPS. Listen to your rider. Keep them informed about what is happening throughout the drive. The best practice here is to simply keep your GPS within view AT ALL TIMES. This way they can see WHY you are going a certain direction, how much longer they have, and if they see something they want to change, they can advise you ahead of time.

Know your limits

One major issue I come across in riding with Lyft is that many drivers do not know their own limitations. This is especially true with older drivers. If you are tired, stop driving. If you don't see well at night, don't drive at night. If you are not a confident driver, you shouldn't drive at all. With Lyft you are going to be placed in a lot of situations that you simply cannot control. If you are someone that has high anxiety, has confidence issues, or has any type of physical limitation, you probably shouldn't drive. Keep in mind these are real people that will be injured really bad if you make bad decisions and you will really be sued. It isn't worth taking the risk just to make a few extra dollars.

It is also important to point out that those that do not speak the local language probably shouldn't drive in that area. This is a big issue that is brought up regularly by my passengers. If they are unable to communicate with their driver it can be a terrifying experience, especially if that driver isn't going the right direction. With the number of times a driver will have to communicate directly with passengers in regards to pickup / drop-off it would be very difficult to drive for Lyft with a language barrier and will likely result in being rated poorly. Since your rating is critical to getting more rides, it is very important that everything be done to protect this rating. If you know that language is going to be an issue, you should consider driving in areas that have a higher concentration of drivers that speak your native language.

Go with the flow

I cannot stress enough that as a driver sometimes you just have to bite your tongue. It doesn't matter how wrong your passenger may be it isn't a good idea to start a war inside of your small vehicle. Brush it off if you can. If you can't, get the passenger out of your vehicle as quickly and safely as possible. Religion, politics, and a number of controversial topics will come up throughout the course of driving. It is important to recognize when a discussion is appropriate and when it is just going to create problems. Sometimes it is easier/safer just to let the passenger blab away while you get them to their destination. If you aren't good at keeping your mouth shut, you won't be driving long.

It is also important to recognize that you are working even though you are in your own vehicle. If you wouldn't say it to a client/customer in any other job, don't say it while driving for Lyft. The same is true when it comes to flirting with passengers. Just don't do it! I don't care if your passenger is your dream man/woman. Let them go! There is nothing more uncomfortable than being trapped inside of a small space with someone that you are not interested in that doesn't seem to get it. It is also a bad idea to touch your passengers. It doesn't matter if your culture kisses on the cheek or believes in touching. Don't do it. It freaks many people out.

It is also a bad idea to make assumptions about your rider. I was picked up by a driver on a Sunday morning to head to business brunch. I was of course dressed up which the driver assumed meant that I was going to church. This turned into a long ride with the driver basically preaching to me. When I attempted to change course in the conversation, he kept bringing it back to the bible, the lord, and everything else religion. At some point I finally advised him that I was not a Christian which led to him being incredibly offended. He then spent the next thirty minutes telling me why I needed to go to church. Needless to say it was an incredibly uncomfortable ride.

The point here is that while you may have opinions, while driving, you don't. The passenger is going to say a lot of things that will make you feel uncomfortable or try to incite you, especially while they are drunk. You have to remember that you are getting paid to provide a service. Your opinion isn't necessary. You can still talk and communicate with your customer without turning your car into a warzone. It just isn't worth it. If the topic is inflammatory, change it. Don't let the customer pull you into a trap. You have to remember that some customers will purposely troll you in order to get your response on video. Don't let yourself get caught up in a viral video because you couldn't keep your mouth shut.

Know the area you are driving in

I have never understood why drivers will go to areas they know nothing about to drive. If you don't know anything about an area, you probably shouldn't be there. This doesn't mean you have to have an intimate first-hand knowledge of every area you wish to drive. It does however mean that you should at least make an attempt to learn about different restaurants, night life, and entertainment options in the major areas you intend on driving. Yes, I am saying that you should do some level of research! This not only reassures your passenger that you aren't an idiot, it can also validate your worth. If you do nothing but drive, you deserve nothing but driver pay. If you become a tour guide and help the passenger learn about the area, find new restaurants, and essentially provide them the experience they expect, you are much more likely to get tips.

I hear a lot of stories about drivers that drive the wrong way down a road, get lost, or get struck in easily avoidable construction zones. If you know the area that you drive in, this isn't going to be a problem. If you want to drive an area, learn about it. Learning about it while you have a passenger in your vehicle is not ideal for you or the passenger.

When/Where should I drive?

One of the main reasons why drivers fail with Lyft is because they don't know HOW to drive. This doesn't mean that they are unable to stay in the lanes or follow directions. It means that they don't know when/where to drive. Understanding this is ultimately what will determine whether you are making $8/hour or more than $20/hour. I realize that Lyft is typically touting returns of $20-$30/hour, but this isn't something that you automatically make. It takes a considerable amount of time to learn how to drive before you'll ever achieve results such as that on a regular basis.

The airport. Why? Why not!

Knowing where and when to drive is heavily dependent upon your knowledge of an area. This is another reason why knowing your area is so important. For most new riders the first place they head to is the airport. While this is a great idea in theory, it isn't the best one. The airport can be both good and bad at the same time. The biggest issue with the airport is the downtime. When you drive to the airport you are automatically placed into a queue. This queue can be big or small, but you don't really know your total wait until you get there and actually start waiting. What I have found is that more often than not, you are going to wait at least 30-45 minutes but at times it could be well over an hour. The problem is that you have to stay at the airport in order to stay in the queue. This means that for 30-45 minutes or longer you are sacrificing the opportunity to get other rides. You are doing this on the assumption that you are going to pick up someone from the airport and have to drive them a long distance.

The reality of airport rides is that they are very unpredictable. You are just as likely to get a long ride as you are to get an incredibly short one. If you get a short one, you would have just waited all that time to get paid $3.50. You then go back to the end of the queue if you'd like to get another ride. Had you just drove around town without the downtime, you would have more than likely made more money, especially if you were able to hit a surge during that time.

The airport is however good if you have other things that you are trying to do at the same time that aren't time sensitive. For example, you really want to read a book but you are willing to take rides between chapters. Maybe you are working on your homework but you want to give yourself random breaks. This is when airport rides can be a good thing. However, if you are waiting for rides and actively ready to drive airports are only worthwhile if the queue is extremely small. In order to see the queue, you can simply click on it at any time from map view. When you click on the icon it will tell you how many cars are in the queue, which can help you determine if it is worth hanging out at the airport or not.

The good thing about the airport is that it is reliable. You will always be able to pick up a ride at the airport. If you are having a slow night but need to make a certain amount of money before you can quit, head to the airport. Some money is better than no money and you never know, you may get lucky and get a super long ride.

Think like the rider

The best way to determine where to go is to think like a rider. If you were going to request a ride, how would you do it? From where? At what time? Knowing how to think like a rider is how the good drivers are able to make considerably more than the bad ones.

During the day, you have to consider things like, when do people go to work? When do they go to lunch? When do they get off work? At night, you must consider when people go out to dinner? When do the malls close? When do people go out to party?

When do the bars close? It is also a good idea to know what time flights DEPART from the airport. For example, in the Tampa region most flights leave the airport between 6 AM and 8 AM. This means that most passengers are going to need rides to the airport between 4 AM and 6 AM. Other considerations include knowing when sporting events will start/end, concerts, festivals/fairs, etc.

Knowing when to be where will help you get the most rides and hit the highest surge areas at the right time. I will typically map out my day before heading out and keep a schedule in front of me so that I stick to it. In order to better illustrate this, I have included a sample schedule that I may use on a typical Saturday night.

Sample Schedule :

5 PM : Start Driving. I will typically start NEAR residential areas that have an abundance of restaurants nearby.

5-7 PM : Dinners runs

7-8 PM : Transition. This is when I will eat, get gas (even if I don't really need it), and use the bathroom. Don't waste your busy times doing this. During this time I will typically mull around the restaurants picking up late leavers.

8-10 PM : Hang out near malls. Most malls close around 9 PM, most employees get out of work 30 minutes after that.

10 PM to 12 PM : Transition to night travel. This is the time you are taking people to their night destinations (bars, clubs, etc).

Midnight to 4 AM : Picking up the drinkers, smokers, etc.

4 AM to 6 AM : Airport runs.

The key to the above schedule is KNOWING the area you are driving in. What I see a lot of drivers doing is hanging out downtown or around the bars at 8 PM. WHY? People aren't leaving the bars at 8 PM, they are heading to the bars around that time. For this reason it makes more sense to drive near high population areas as that is most likely going to be where the ride will START. The same is true with going out to eat. Why would you hang out by the restaurants when the passengers are going to be leaving from their homes? Hanging out by the restaurants, malls, or places where people are attempting to go to will ensure you have nothing but short rides. If you go a little further out to high population centers, you'll ensure you are getting longer rides as they need to travel further to get to their destinations.

When doing airport runs you need to consider distance. If you hang out near the airport, the only airport runs you will get are the short ones. Airport runs are really only worthwhile if they are a decent distance away from the airport. To accomplish this, I will typically do most of my pickups near bars until 4 AM. At this point in time I will start driving home and pickup any rides along the way, knowing that from 4 AM to 6 AM it is highly likely some of those rides will be airport runs. If I am able to make it all the way home without getting a ride, I will typically end my night. Since my drive home is typically 30-45 minutes from my last drop off, it is very rare that I make it home without another ride. Keep in mind that the best times for airport runs may be very different in your area than in mine. For this reason it is important to do your research to help you understand when you should drive where.

The key is being where the drivers are at any period of time. If they are at home, go there. If they are out, go there. Going where you are most likely to find requests just makes logical sense but too often drivers don't recognize this and will sit in areas where the riders want to go, rather than where they actually are. Sure you will get rides in those areas, but you are more likely to get longer, better paying rides by going where the demand is going to be.

Playing the surge

Surge pricing is where a driver can make significantly more money than usual for doing the same work. The surge price is controlled by the amount of demand as compared to the supply of drivers. This will normally happen during major sporting events, festivals, or closing time in a known party district.

There are two major strategies when it comes to surges. You can either go directly to the source of the surge OR you can drive the outskirts of the surge and take advantage of surge pricing without the chaos of going to the epicenter of the surge. Either of these options can provide nice returns, but I have found that often I will do better just outside of the epicenter as I am able to take more rides faster than I can by getting trapped in the traffic created by the surge source. This is especially true with events that end at a specific time such as a sporting event or a concert. If you go directly to the stadium, you may drive around for a while looking for your passenger, then you get caught in traffic. By working the outer bands of the surge, I still get surge pricing but instead of having to find my passenger in a sea of 50k people, I can just pick them up at the front of a bar with maybe 10 people. I also avoid a lot of the traffic associated with those popular events. This normally results in my ability to transport numerous rides with surge pricing compared to maybe doing a single ride at surge by going directly to the source. The risk is that you put yourself too far outside of the main surge source or are in an area where people will simply wait out the surge altogether. When this happens you will have missed out on a surge opportunity altogether.

When it comes to a surge it is important to recognize that they do not last forever. In fact, most surges are VERY short lived. For this reason unless you are very close to that area it really isn't worth chasing the surge. By knowing the local area, knowing the events, and having a strategy in place when you start your shift you are more likely to hit surge pricing than you would without a plan. For example, you know that the bars get out in a popular party district at 3 AM, you should probably get to that area around that time to take advantage of the surge. If a surge never happens at least you'll be in an area where you would be more likely to get passengers.

If you plan on taking advantage of a surge, consider a few things before heading towards the surge. Don't accept any rides that are outside of the surge area when you are in it. This is an easy way to miss out on a surge completely. In an area that you know is going to be busy at a certain time such as a sporting event or concert, keep your app off until AFTER the surge hits. By turning your app on too early you'll miss the highest point of the surge which happens shortly after the end of an event. You have to give a few minutes for the demand to build up first. This could make a major difference if you have a far that is normally $20 and you take a 4x surge to make $80 or if you take a 1.5x surge and end up with $30. By timing the surge properly in this scenario it would have made a difference of $50. Often events are going to draw in people from areas that are much further away than your typical ride. Take advantage of these longer trips, especially when there is a surge.

What times should I drive?

The time of day and the actual physical days you drive can make a major difference on your hourly rate. While you can make money any day of the week, the better you understand the "flow" of the week, the better opportunity you will have to make GOOD money.

Just like everything else, it is important to understand how the rider thinks. For example, a rider isn't thinking about going to bars between 9-5 during the week. Just like most riders aren't thinking about going to work between 10 PM and 2 AM on the weekends. Obviously there are those that work and play outside of the "typical" hours for these activities, but the majority tend to follow certain standard hours for activities.

If you are trying to plan a schedule to work, you have to really think about WHEN and HOW people are planning to ride. Many drivers want to drive 9 AM to 5 PM but then complain that they aren't making any money. Why? Well, if you drive during the hours that others are working, you aren't going to have as many rides. A better shift would be to work 4 AM to 2 PM if you want to work an 8 hour shift during the morning. Doing this shift will allow you to pickup airport runs from 4 AM to 6 AM (assuming your airport does mostly early morning departments), you would then take people to work from 6 AM to 9 AM, 9 AM to 11 AM you are shuttling people to doctor's appointments, and from 11 AM to 2 PM you would be running passengers to lunch.

If you are trying to work a later shift, then a good start time would be 5:00 PM with and time of 1 AM (during the week) and a start time of 6:30 PM with an end time of 4 AM on weekends (Friday/Saturday). If you are working Sundays, you should try to work for morning church and brunch at a minimum, which is typically 7 AM to 3 PM.

If you are a night person, you can run the best shift of all. Working from 9 PM to 6 AM is a fantastic shift. The rides are typically longer as you aren't getting as many people trying to go to the store or work or anywhere local. The best part though is that you have significantly less traffic and much less competition from other drivers. Sure you may have greater downtime, but often times you make up for it in the lack of stress, the lower gas costs from idling, and the longer rides that you will typically see.

As you can see, you can't simply turn on the app and expect to make money, you really have to consider where people are going to be, what is happening, and formulate a plan that will work well within those guidelines. This doesn't mean that you have to stick to these hours. You can do split shifts, you can work less, you can work more, or you could just create whatever hours you want and hope for the best. These hours however are the ones that will give you a full shift that is consistently good. The goal of course is to set yourself up with the greatest possible outcome. Sometimes doing that means working slightly outside of the hours you would typically want to work.

Holidays, Holidays, Holidays

If you want to make real money off of ride share, you have to work holidays. Not only are more passengers using Lyft during this time period, you also have less competition as other drivers are going to take these days off. It is the perfect combination to create surge pricing.

So what holidays matter most? The holidays that are the best are normally going to be the ones that involve drinking. This is especially true on New Years, 4th of July, St Patricks Day, Cinco De Mayo, and during Christmas as the Christmas parties start to ramp up. On these days you can typically make 2-3x more than you would during a similar day without a holiday. People also tend to tip better during the holidays, especially around the Christmas season.

Weekends "vs" Weekdays

Do you enjoy having weekends off? Did you pick up Lyft because you wanted to work less on the weekend and have more control of your schedule? You should probably reconsider. There is a dramatic difference between working during the week and working during the weekend. This is especially true if you work Friday and Saturday night. These are by far the best days of the week to work. Cutting them out of your schedule is a fantastic way to dramatically reduce your weekly earnings. Again, you have to drive when riders need rides.

So when should I drive?

Nights, weekends, and holidays! You thought this was going to give you more flexibility? Yes, it does, but that doesn't mean you'll have more flexibility in your social life. Making money with Lyft relies heavily on your willingness to drive when everyone else is out partying. If you enjoy the night life, like having holidays off, and like to sleep in, you are cutting out the best possible hours for making money. Just because the hours are 100% flexible, doesn't mean that flexibility is profitable.

High Ratings, Higher Tips

Initially I considered having a section for ratings and a separate one for tips, but realized that they really go hand in hand. The reality is that if you are good enough to get 5 stars, you should be good enough to earn a tip. There is however a major difference in what some drivers earn, especially when it comes to tips.

One thing that stops many drivers from earning tips is their inability to be more than "just a driver". They are more focused on the destination than that ride itself. They may be police, they may follow directions well, the music is good, and overall they provide a good experience, but they just aren't "tip worthy". The major difference between a tip worthy driver and any other driver is the "experience". The drivers that earn the most tips are willing to go above and beyond to make each and every ride memorable. This can be done in a number of different ways, but in order to earn tips consistently you need to be willing to go above and beyond on EVERY ride.

How should I dress?

Believe it or not, the way that you dress can have a major impact on not only your rating but the likelihood you'll get a tip. This is especially true if your ride is going out for a special event such as an anniversary dinner, a birthday, or any type of celebration. If they are dressed nice but you look like a bum, you could be the greatest driver in the world but your attire will take away from the special event. This doesn't mean that you have to wear a full suit, but wearing a polo or button up shirt can go a long way towards creating a positive experience for the rider.

Your dress needs to go beyond just your clothing. It also means that you should probably take a shower before driving, wear deodorant, brush your teeth, and overall present yourself in a clean manner. Having your hair messed up like you just rolled out of bed is less than inspiring to your rider. Wearing shorts and a t shirt may be your style, but you look like you work this job because nobody else will give you one. The goal should be to look like you could work anywhere, but you choose to do ride share. Even wearing pants with a polo and combing your hair can make a dramatic difference in how you are perceived. Just take the time to make yourself look professional.

What should be on the radio?

There really isn't a secret sauce for radio. I find that the best option is always the path of least resistance. This normally means listening to Top 40 or POP music. It is called POP music because it is popular. It has the greatest appeal. I have found that the Rap/Hip Hop and Country are probably the two worst types of music to play as riders typically either hate them or love them. Top 40 is generally accepted as reasonable music to listen to in the car even if it is not their normal preferred style of music.

Another option of course is to find out what your riders would like to listen to. This of course can be both good and bad. I have had customers that are pretty easy going with their music and those that want some of the most obscure music possible. This also opens the door to riders requesting to Bluetooth into your vehicle or connect via aux cable.

The important thing to remember is that music can drive the mood inside the car. If your passengers are going to a party, they typically want to feel like it. It may be your car, but while you have passengers, it is their experience. Just because you want to listen to the basketball game, doesn't mean that your passenger does. Be smart and drive the mood. Mood can create great opportunity for tips.

What about snacks? Drinks? Mints? Chargers?

The use of snacks, drinks, mints, etc has been somewhat of a long debate with many drivers. The problem is that these types of items come with a very real cost but rarely do they produce any real reward. Sure a customer may appreciate it and rate you higher because they feel it adds to their experience, but does it add to the "value". In reality it adds greater cost which means you would need to earn significantly more in tips to offset that additional expense.

I have found that the drivers that do the best with snacks are those that aren't great with creating conversation. In fact, this can often times become a conversation starter. I do however have a better option that will be both a conversation starter, a value builder, and a revenue driver.

Instead of offering your passenger FREE snacks, you can simply ask the passenger if they would like to make any additional stops on the way to their destination. This can be a good way to start conversation with a customer, it shows them that you are looking out for them, and if they do stop you get paid for the time that you are idling at the gas station waiting for them. I realize that for some drivers hate "idling" because we get paid the most when we are actively creating miles. The reality is that a stop at a gas station feels to the rider like you are doing them a favor not to mention it gives them a chance to get cash, make change, etc. I get more tips when my passengers stop at a gas station because they now have the ability to tip me $5 instead of the $20 that they have in their pocket.

Mints are probably the only item that I keep in my vehicle for FREE. I find that offering mints is incredibly inexpensive and has the same level of satisfaction as offering a snack or water.

Another way that you can enhance the level of service in your vehicle without increasing your cost is to offer free WiFi through your phone if you are able to operate a hot spot with unlimited data. You can even add stickers on your windows stating that you offer WiFi. Hand in hand with the WiFi should be a way for your customers to charge their phones. I get asked for a charger more often than anything else. I highly recommend keeping a multi phone adapter in your vehicle so that your riders can charge their phones regardless of the type of phone charger they need. Having these two service options available can make customers happy without increasing your cost.

How often should I clean? What about fragrance?

If you want tips, especially from women you have to have a clean vehicle. This is easily one of the biggest complains I hear about other drivers. I hear that the vehicle was dirty or smelled funny. This is also the easiest thing to control. There is absolutely no reason why you shouldn't have an immaculate vehicle every time you start driving.

So how often should you clean your vehicle? EVERY DAY! If you are going to drive, you should clean your vehicle first. This doesn't just mean hitting the car wash, it means a full vacuum. Does it sound expensive? It can be. Many areas offer monthly car wash packages for a flat fee. I pay $30/month and I can wash my car and vacuum it as many times as I want.

Besides just visible cleanliness, your vehicle has to smell great too. This doesn't mean it should smell like perfume/cologne. It means it should smell like something that the average person finds appealing. Avoid smells like vanilla which can trigger headaches and opt for something a little more subtle and relaxing such as sage or citrus. The smell of your vehicle is not a once a day consideration, it should be reevaluated after each ride.

Another major issue is smoking. For someone that is a smoker, this may not seem like a big deal, but for a non-smoker, it is absolutely wretched. If you smoke, don't do it in your vehicle that you use for Lyft, especially between rides. It is incredibly difficult to get the smell of smoke out of a vehicle and it is an easy way to get a low rating. You may not be able to smell it, but a non-smoker can easily spot it no matter how much you spray your car. You are going to have people ask if they can smoke in your vehicle, you should always tell them no. Just because you don't care, doesn't mean that the next passenger won't. I have done thousands of rides and I have never had a passenger freak out because I wouldn't let them smoke in my vehicle, but I have heard many complain about the smell of smokes in other vehicles.

Opening Doors for customers?

Opening the door for your customers can seem like a simple gesture that would be universally seen as good customer service, but it really isn't. When I first started ride share, I would open the door for everyone. It didn't take long for me to find out why this isn't the best idea.

Opening the door sends different messages to different people. Some will find it in good taste, while others will be offended by the idea that you believe they need your help with a door. I have found that it is generally just safer to not open any doors unless the customer has some sort of a physical disability and they request your assistance. I have never had someone upset about my not opening a door, but I have had enough people that seemed put off by the idea that I decided a while ago to stop opening doors altogether.

So how do I get higher tips?

Getting higher tips will come from a combination of all of your efforts. If you create great conversation, your vehicle is clean/smells good, you stopped so they could buy some cigs, and you ultimately created a great overall experience the customer is more likely to give you a tip.

The best way to look at getting a tip is whether or not you made a friend. If you feel that your connection with the customer was good enough that you could see yourself hanging out with them in a bar, the likelihood that you'll get a tip is dramatically increased. The goal should always be to create an experience that is outside of the ordinary Lyft ride. You should always strive for the rider to state out loud that it was an excellent ride, that you were hilarious, or that they really enjoyed speaking with you. Again, it is all about creating a top notch experience that is above and beyond what they expected.

Another way to generate more tips is to find ways to bring them up in conversation without directly asking for them. For example, a customer could ask how your night is going, and you could say that it has been a good night for tips. You aren't directly asking for money but you are putting the idea of tipping in their head. This is especially important if you are driving with Uber which doesn't allow riders the option to tip inside of the app. With Lyft many riders will round up their fare in order to give a tip. The hope is that they will not only round it but add a few dollars to it as well.

If you are driving at night an easy way to get a tip is to ask the rider if they need to make any stops on way. If they just got done drinking, there's a good chance this will prompt them to stop for food. Of all of the times I have stopped for food, rarely am I not offered something to eat. In fact many riders insist on it. Don't take advantage of this offer by ordering something ridiculous. Just keep it simple, grab a burger, maybe a taco. If it isn't something you have to pay for that you normally would, even a free burger or taco can be a tip. Sometimes you'll still get a normal tip on top of the food that you ordered. It is all about creating a connection with your passenger first and they will be excited to treat you to a free meal.

Taxes, Taxes, Taxes!

This section isn't going to be long, but I made a separate section to show the importance of it. I cannot stress enough how important taxes are to your overall income. The problem is that the vast majority of drivers, even the seasoned ones look at taxes the wrong way. Taxes when it comes to ride share are a very good thing. In fact, taxes are so good that you can make more money from your taxes than you can off of driving at times. The key is that you have to understand how taxes work when it comes to ride share.

Most drivers see taxes as something they have to pay. The better way to look at taxes is that you get paid 53.5 cents per mile that you drive. This means every mile you drive with the customer in your car, every mile you drive while going to get a customer, and every mile that you drive while trying to acquire business. Do the math. This can be a significant amount of money over time especially if you focus on the longer rides.

So how do you make money from ride share? Through your taxes! Do yourself a favor and download an app that will calculate your miles for you and put them into a printable report and you'll be set. I personally like MileIQ. You pay a small fee for it, but it will keep track of your rides automatically through GPS which you will then classify as either personal or business related. At the end of the year, you print out the documents and include them with your taxes. It is literally that simple. This is why I don't use dollar goals when I drive like most drivers. I use mileage goals. I know that I'll make money by driving miles, but I will also get a huge tax credit by driving as many miles as possible.

This is where I am going to state that you should still speak with a tax professional in regards to your taxes and how the mileage credits work.

Insurance, Fuel, Expenses

One of the biggest concerns when driving should always be your expenses. The reality is that you are going to have a lot more expenses than you realize and you have to budget for them or you could find yourself without money and without a way to earn more.

How does insurance work?

The biggest expense that you are typically going to have will be your insurance. Yes, Lyft does provide insurance while you are on a ride but you have to realize that the act of driving for Lyft will immediately nullify your personal insurance policy. It doesn't matter if you are driving once a week or full time. You cannot do Uber and have a personal insurance policy. This is the easiest way to have claims rejected. I have seen many drivers have this issue when they tried to file a claim and ultimately the insurance company determined they were using their vehicle for ride share.

Another problem with insurance is that while you are technically covered while you are driving for Lyft, you aren't protected while you are driving to pick-up your passengers. This is where the personal policy fails to meet the needs of a ride share driver.

So what type of policy should you carry? Technically anyone that is driving for Lyft should have either a commercial policy OR a rideshare policy. This doesn't necessarily mean that your rates are going to be significantly higher than what you currently pay, but it is important to have the right type of insurance to make certain you are covered if you were to get into an accident. Rideshare policies are somewhat new and create an option that is somewhere between a commercial policy and a personal one. Currently the major provider of rideshare policies is a company called Foremost.

Yes, having the right type of policy is going to cost you more than you are currently paying but if you are going to do it, you need to do it right. No sense paying for a policy that won't even pay out if you were to actually need it.

Fuel

Obviously while driving you are going to need more fuel than you would in your day to day usage. Fuel is typically going to be one of the biggest ride share expenses. While you are able to control the amount of fuel you use to some degree, you can't control it completely.

One of the easiest ways to control the amount of fuel that you use is to be more efficient in your driving. This means only driving when you have someone in your vehicle. For some this means turning off their vehicle completely until you have a ride. For others this means finding a spot to wait for rides and idling until you have someone to pickup. The problem with both of these methods is that while you may save on fuel, you may also sacrifice on rides. In my personal experience, I have received far more rides while in motion on a roadway than I do while sitting idle in a parking lot. This is something that needs to be balanced but I prefer to stay moving and figure I will make up the additional expense by claiming the miles on my taxes. It is all about personal preference.

Fuel cards are another way to reduce your expenses. I personally prefer Racetrac although their app isn't the most reliable. The app allows me to get points based on my fuel and store purchases. I can then take those points and exchange them for free store merchandise. They also have a tiered system based on the amount of points that you earn. With each tier you earn additional free fountain drinks. The free drinks can range from one free drink per month on up to getting one free drink per day. I have reached the "Sultan of Soda" tier, which is the highest. I am now able to get one free medium drink a day for free for a year. Drinks are a major expense for a driver so this is an added benefit from something that I have to purchase anyway. I suggest enrolling in these types of rewards programs with several different gas stations. If you are going to spend the money anyway you might as well get additional perks. Other gas stations that I get perks from are Thorntons and WaWa. Each company has slightly different perks but with the number of miles you drive with Lyft, these perks add up quickly.

Maintenance

This is where a lot of drivers get in major trouble. If you are relying on Lyft for income and something happens to your vehicle, you are essentially out of business. Since Lyft will not allow you to use a rental car, you have no choice but to get your vehicle up and running again. This is why it is incredibly important to plan ahead when it comes to maintenance.

I suggest taking 15% of all earnings and throw it into a separate account. This account should never be touched unless you need the money for maintenance. I realize 15% sounds like a lot, but all it takes is one major event to knock you out of business and you'll wish you were following this guideline when that happens. You have to remember that as a driver you should expect to get new tires and brake pads annually, oil changes monthly, and a number of other repairs throughout the time you own the vehicle. By setting aside money you'll be able to get back on the road quickly when major events happen and you won't have the financial constrains that many drivers face when these events happen. I have known many drivers that stopped driving simply because their car broke down and they didn't have the money to fix it. The problem is that if you have a major repair but don't have the money, you no longer have the ability to drive to earn that additional money. You are effectively shut down. Don't let this happen to you, plan ahead.

Cell Phone

This should be one of the first bills you pay each month. If you don't have your phone, you don't have Lyft. It is that simple. You also need a plan just in case your phone breaks, gets lost, or is stolen. Again, without your phone, you aren't driving for Lyft. A good friend of mine and fellow driver is terrible at paying his cell phone bill and is constantly shut down for a few days while he figures out a way to pay his bill. With any other bill you can simply Lyft more to get the money but you can't do that if you don't have access to Lyft. Be smart, pay your cell phone bill!

Cost reduction!

One of the fastest ways to fail as a driver is by letting your expenses pile up. Too many drivers will go to a gas station to buy energy drinks, go out to eat several times throughout their day, and will buy snacks for the road. The problem is that by doing so you are spending significantly more for food than you would if you would simply pack your lunch. Do the math and you'll see just how much you are spending in a day by eating out.

If you are able and willing, clean your own vehicle. You just have to make certain that you are doing it well and regularly. I personally prefer spending the $30 for a monthly cleaning package at the local car wash which comes with free vacuums. This may not be an option in your area. If you enjoy cleaning your own vehicle and have some free time, this is definitely an area where you can cut expenses. Don't cut out cleaning altogether or do it less frequently as this is more likely to hurt you than help you.

Safety, Puke Avoidance, and more

Next to making money, this is probably the most important section of the entire book. I cannot stress enough how incredibly important it is to be safe while driving. After doing thousands of rides, I have mostly had good experiences but those few bad situations remind me how important safety is.

How to stay safe

The most important thing that you need to remember about Lyft is that YOU CAN REJECT ANY RIDE. Let me repeat that, YOU CAN REJECT ANYRIDE. There is nothing racist about refusing to go to a bad neighborhood. This doesn't make you a bad person. This doesn't make you judgmental. I realize that the majority of people in bad areas are probably good people, but if you don't feel comfortable driving in those areas, don't. You have 100% control of this. Don't feel obligated to go to those parts of town if you simply feel on edge while you are there. It just isn't worth it. Turn off the app and move somewhere that feels safer.

This is also true for riders. If you go to pick up a rider and they look aggressive, overly drunk, possibly high, don't pick them up. You have the right to drive past them and cancel the ride. It is your obligation to yourself to stay safe. Lyft does not provide drivers with any protection from riders. It is our own responsibility to make good judgment calls when it comes to our passengers.

If you feel you have someone in your car that is questionable, the best thing you can do is keep calm and do your best not to set them off. Just get them to their destination, get them out of your vehicle, and move on. Once they are in your vehicle kicking them out is almost impossible and probably much more dangerous than simply driving them where they need to go. Setting someone off inside a confined space while you are driving and unable to defend yourself is never a good idea.

You will also experience passengers that are going to want to drink in the vehicle, smoke in the vehicle, and even some that will bring small children into your vehicle without a car seat. It is your responsibility to tell them no. It isn't worth getting a ticket or going to jail because you are allowing someone you don't even know to do something illegal in your vehicle. You have to be the one in control of the situation. You are the driver, it is your car, so it is your responsibility to ensure that your passengers are following the rules. Don't let them dictate what will be done.

In addition to the passengers you pick up you have to be aware of where you are at any given time. You have to remember that there is a chance that your car could become disabled in any area at any moment. Knowing where you are can go a long way towards ensuring you remain safe. It may also change your thinking when you decide to take that extremely rough street to cut a minute off your drive.

What about weapons?

I am going to address personal defense as diplomatically as possible. Typically weapons for personal defense are not allowed in your vehicle while driving for Lyft. If the passenger was to see one it could be reason enough for you to get banned from Lyft. There is however a dramatic difference between what Lyft would like you to do and what actually happens.

I am friends with quite a few other drivers and have had conversations with many others. One of the biggest conversations is in regards to self-defense. The big question is whether or not we carry weapons with us in the vehicle for protection. The overwhelming response is YES. Does this go against Lyft policy, definitely. The argument has always been that Lyft isn't the one that is getting stabbed, we are. The other argument is that it is our own personal vehicle and we are allowed by our state to carry, so Lyft has no jurisdiction in those matters. While these are valid arguments it has always been a somewhat taboo topic. As a corporate entity Lyft almost has to take a strong stance against weapons in the vehicle just as most employers do. It is a huge liability issue for obvious reasons.

The best I can do is tell you to do what you feel is the best option for you and your family within the guidelines of the law with Lyft policy in consideration. Just be smart and do what you need to do in order to feel more comfortable while driving for Lyft. I will however make a recommendation to definitely not use pepper spray in your vehicle unless you enjoy disabling yourself.

Puke Avoidance

I have done thousands of rides with the vast majority at night and on weekends when passengers are typically very intoxicated. With so many drunk passengers I am very proud to say that I have only had ONE person throw up INSIDE of my vehicle. I will get into the details of the person that did puke in my car later as I knew it was going to happen.

When it comes to picking up riders, again, you CAN REJECT RIDE REQUESTS. My fellow driver friends report puke incidents in their vehicles on a regular basis. It is my belief that puke incidents are almost 100% avoidable if you understand how to avoid them.

Any time I accept a ride, especially in an area that is known to be a "party" location, I make certain I inspect the passengers BEFORE unlocking my doors. I want to know what is getting in my car before I actually let them in. If I notice that the passenger is heavily swaying, burping, or has the "sweats" then I will decline the ride advising them to sit down and relax for a bit first.

I realize is mainly utilized by those that are too drunk to drive. I do believe there is also a point where someone is too drunk to ride. Lyft is paying me to "share" my ride with passengers. They aren't paying me as an employee. They aren't providing the vehicle. I am not willing to sacrifice my own vehicle to make sometimes as long as $3.50 for a trip. Yes, you can get paid if someone does puke in your vehicle, but I assure you the expense of cleaning puke out of a vehicle is significantly greater than what you get. When someone pukes in your vehicle, you are done for the day, possibly for several days. Normally the smell is so strong that it takes several days of cleaning/airing out to get rid of it. If they manage to puke inside of cracks and crevices it could take a lot of man hours trying to remove panels to remove it all. It is a very time consuming process. Don't forget that while you are cleaning the vehicle and airing it out you are unable to drive people around which costs even more money. The cleaning fee will never be adequate enough to cover the cost of someone puking in your car.

It is almost impossible to completely avoid getting someone in your car that could potentially puke at any moment. For this reason it is important to understand puking. If you know someone is possibly on the edge, MAKE THEM sit up front. People are significantly less likely to puke when they are sitting up front. Adding motion sickness to the equation is never going to help the problem and if you remember feeling sick in the backseat as a kid you know what I'm talking about. Once they are in the front seat, make the vehicle as cold as the passenger can handle, preferably with the windows down. No idea why this works but it does. Finally, avoid major roadways. It is very difficult to pull off to the side of the road for them to puke if you are going 70 MPH. Side roads will allow you to drive slowly enough that you can get over, unlock the doors, and they can get the door open in time. Finally, you need to be patient and reassuring. If you make them feel guilty about stopping, they are going to stop asking and will puke in your vehicle. Don't force someone to be a hero. If they puke in the car because you were too aggressive with them, that is your fault.

www.ingramcontent.com/pod-product-compliance
Lightning Source LLC
Chambersburg PA
CBHW061230180526
45170CB00003B/1231